CW00447107

Introduction
Shorthaired Breeds
American Shorthair
American Wirehair
British and European Shorthai
Exotic Shorthair   15
Japanese Bobtail   16
Manx and Cymric   17
Rex   18
Scottish Fold and American Curl   19
Snowshoe   20
Sphynx   21
Longhaired Breeds
Birman and Ragdoll   22
Maine Coon   23
Norwegian Forest   24
Peke-faced Persian   25
Persian (Longhaired)   26
Turkish Angora   29
Turkish Van   30
Oriental Breeds
Abyssinian and Somali   31
Burmese and Malayan   33
Egyptian Mau   35
Havana Brown   36
Korat   37
Ocicat and Bengali   38
Oriental (Foreign) Shorthair   39
Russian Blue   40
Siamese   41
Balinese and Javanese   43
Singapura and Bombay   44
Tonkinese   45
The New Breeds   46

INTRODUCTION

The domestic cat we know today is a form of the small wild cat, *Felis silvestris*, from North Africa and Europe. Cat bones have been found in excavations at Jericho which date from 6700 B.C. but there is no firm evidence for cats being kept as pets until the time of the Egyptian pharaohs. By 1600 B.C. cats were well-established in Egyptian homes, protected by law and revered for their association with Egyptian gods. From Egypt they were taken to Rome and throughout her Empire. Cats became valued as rodent catchers, but their past association with pagan religion linked them with the devil and led to persecution.

By the 19th century, the popularity of cats was such that cat 'fanciers' began to breed them for their appearance and to show them in competition. The first real cat show was held at the Crystal Palace, London, in 1871, the idea of Harrison Weir, an artist and cat-lover who saw this as an opportunity to draw attention to the existence of different breeds and to encourage good breeding practices. Cat shows were launched in America at Madison Square Garden, New York, in 1895.

In 1887 the National Cat Club was founded in Britain to register pedigree cats and in 1910 nineteen cat clubs met and formed the Governing Council of the Cat Fancy. Today many countries have their own cat organizations which arrange shows, set the standards to which cats of each breed must conform, and give official recognition to new breeds. Of the nine registration bodies in North America, the oldest is the American Cat Association, founded in 1899; the largest is the Cat Fanciers Association. Until 1983 the Governing Council of the Cat Fancy was Britain's only organization. There is now a second, break-away body, the Cat Association of Britain.

A cat's physical characteristics are, of course, determined by the genes it inherits from its parents. Some of these are dominant and some recessive. When a gene for a particular colour, pattern, hair type or physical detail is recessive and is matched with a dominant gene for the same element of the cat's makeup, the effects of the dominant gene will be seen.

Overall, short hair is dominant over long hair and a full coat is dominant over Rex coats, but Manx is dominant over normal tails. Tabby patterning of the fur is dominant over non-tabby, black is dominant over blue and white is dominant over all other colours.

Only when a kitten inherits the same non-dominant gene from both parents will that characteristic appear in its makeup. But although a kitten can show the appearance of a dominant gene, it will still carry the recessive and be able to pass it on to its own offspring.

Of a cat's 38 pairs of chromosomes – which carry the genes – one pair determines gender. Females have two identical X chromosomes and males have one X and one Y. A kitten will inherit an X chromosome from its mother and either an X or a Y from its father thus determining its sex. Some characteristics are sex-linked, i.e. the relevant genes are carried on the sex chromosomes. The red coat colour, its dilute cream forms and the tortoiseshell mixtures of which red and cream form a part are all sex-linked. The gene for red can be carried only on the X chromosome. A male can have a red coat even though it carries only one gene for red, but male tortoiseshells, on the other hand, are theoretically impossible because the tortoiseshell colouring depends upon a combination of two X chromosomes. In fact the occasional male tortoiseshell is born because it has a Y chromosome and two Xs. Such males are almost always sterile.

As well as genes which affect a single characteristic, there are others, known as polygenes, which act together to modify characteristics established by other genes. These can affect coat length and the strength of coat and eye colour.

Another linking which breeders must take into account is that between white fur, blue eyes and deafness. If a pure white cat has blue eyes there is a strong possibility that it will be deaf. However, if there is even a tiny patch of colour in the fur when it is a kitten — even though it disappears later — which would indicate that the cat is not genetically pure white, its hearing is not usually impaired. Sometimes a cat with only one blue eye is deaf in one ear only.

Cat genetics is a complicated subject which is not fully understood and in which there are discoveries still to be made. Anyone wishing to understand the finer points involved should consult a specialist book on the subject.

The various cat registration bodies do not all agree on what should be recognized as distinct cat breeds and when they do may still differ in their ideas of what makes the perfect cat of its type. Anyone wishing to show a cat in competition should consult the body organizing the cat show for the standards which they consider necessary for a cat of any particular breed, though in general they follow the descriptions given here in terms of colour, coat and conformation.

In retrospect the way in which various types and colours became recognized as breeds in the early days of the cat fancy may now seem rather arbitrary and it is not easy to agree on the ways in which cats should be grouped since an arrangement by coat length will produce different divisions from those made according to body type. The arrangement followed here has been to group shorthaired cats originating in Europe and those developing from them together; longhaired cats of European and middle eastern origin are grouped together; and the Siamese and other oriental cats and those developed from them are placed in a third section – the foreign and oriental breeds. Where the United Kingdom associations use a different name for a type of breed from that used in the U.S.A., this appears in brackets after the American name.

AMERICAN SHORTHAIR

Below: Dilute Calico
Right: Cream American Shorthair

Colours: The American Shorthair is recognized in all solid, tabby, patched and tipped coat colours and patterns except for the Siamese pointed-patterned coat. American standards require tortoiseshell to be in well-defined patches; a chestnut tortie is recognized by some associations and several call a tortoiseshell and white a calico – a cat with tri-colour patching (or just red and black) and predominantly white underparts.

In the U.S.A. itself the cat also appears as a blue tabby – not a variety found in British and European shows. The blue-cream has much more defined patches than in Europe. A distinct form of bi-colour, the Van pattern, is also recognized, with solid, tabby or tortoiseshell patching on the head and tail like that of the Turkish Van (page 30) plus isolated patches on the body or limbs.

Description: American Shorthairs developed from cats brought to the U.S.A. from Europe. The first shorthair to be registered with the Cat Fanciers Association was a champion red tabby tom from England with the rather unmasculine name of Belle, while the first 'homegrown' shorthair was Buster Brown, pedigree unknown, who was a male smoke. These and other imported and indigenous cats were all known as Shorthairs and later Domestic Shorthairs. It was not until 1966 that the breed was renamed the American Shorthair and it was decided to allow native American breed non-pedigree cats and kittens to be registered in order to maintain the breed's native American differences.

The American Shorthair is not as square and cobby as the British cat and

its legs are longer. Although the head is large with full cheeks, it is longer than it is wide giving an oblong rather than a rounded look. The ears are larger, round-tipped and not set so widely apart. The fur of the American Shorthair is thick and hard compared with the soft resilience of the British coat. Its eyes are large, round and set well apart, giving a particularly open look. They are copper or deep gold with most fur colours, though blue or odd-eyed with solid colour white. The Silver Patched Tabby may also have hazel eyes, while the Chinchillas and other tipped cats have emerald or aquamarine eyes and the Silver Tabby, green or hazel.

The Silver Tabby, in which the black tabby markings overlay a coat which is coloured at the tips of the fur to produce a sparkling silvery effect, is perhaps the best known of the American Shorthairs, in classic or mackerel form. In young kittens its tabby markings are often somewhat muted but as they grow they become very handsome cats.

Below: Van pattern
Left: Brown-patched Silver Tabby

AMERICAN WIREHAIR

Below: Calico Wirehair
Right: Tabby Wirehair

Colours: American Wirehairs are acceptable in all the colours and patterns recognized for the American Shorthair: self, bi-colour, tri-colour, patched white, tabby, tipped and smoke but not the pointed pattern. Long-coated kittens are sometimes born with the fur forming real ringlets but it is always coarse and wiry.

Description: There is a record of two cats with wiry fur being found on a British building site and exhibited at the National Cat Club Show in London in the mid-1960s; others have since turned up in Canada, Germany and other places. The American Wirehair, however, developed from Adam, a chance mutation with red and white crimped and wiry hair born on a farm in New York State in 1966. He was mated to one of his normal-coated sisters and the breed was developed.

The original cats were long and slim with longish legs and tall ears but careful breeding with American Shorthairs produced a cat with all the characteristics of the Shorthair, but with more oval paws, and eyes with a slightly upward tilt, yet with the characteristic short and wiry hair.

Colours: British Shorthairs may be self coloured (i.e. solid) black, blue, red, cream, lilac or chocolate; they may also be classic (blotched) or mackerel (striped) tabby. Other types are spotted or bicoloured – white cats patched with any one of the other colours and with the patching always extending over the face and preferably with a white blaze running down over the nose.

In addition there are various tortoiseshells: mixed black, red and cream with no colour dominating any area except for a blaze on the face;

chocolate tortoiseshells and their 'dilute' versions; blue-cream and lilac cream, tabby-marked tortoiseshell (known as 'torbie') or these mixtures patched on white.

Silver, smoke or tipped varieties also exist.

Description: Domestic cats were probably introduced into Britain by the Romans but we do not know what these early cats looked like. Mosaics discovered at Pompei and in Rome show brown striped tabbies, looking very much like the native wild cat of Britain and Europe, which can be distinguished from the domestic cat by its larger size and usually heavier build and by the blunt tip to its tail.

There are striped tabby cats drawn in medieval manuscript margins but a 17th century English writer remarks upon two tabbies presented to Archbishop Laud in 1630 (which he calls 'Cyprus Cats') as though the pattern were unusual, saying that the common English cat was 'white with some blewish piedness' – i.e. white with bluish patches.

Edward Topsell who, in his *History*

Below: Brown Spotted Tabby
Left: British Black

Below: Tortoiseshell and white
Right: British Red Spotted

of *Four-footed Beasts*, published in 1607, offers a mixture of accurate observation and an eclectic range of odd beliefs culled from various sources, describes cats as being of various colours, and includes a woodcut of a striped tabby. He writes of black cats as coming from Spain, but scientific research suggests that they developed in the eastern Mediterranean in classical times. From reference to them in reports of witchcraft and Satanic cults they were well known in Europe by the Middle Ages.

At some time around 1600 the 'blotched' or 'classic' tabby, with whorls of pattern on its sides instead of tiger stripes, seems to have appeared in Britain. It spread from there up the rivers of western Europe which were English trading routes and later with British colonists to other parts of the world, though the same pattern also developed in the Middle East. Both

types of tabby now have to conform to very strict requirements for pedigree breeds, with stripes along the spine, barred legs and tail, and markings across the cheeks and on the forehead. At the same time the grey coat colour – if it is the colour which cat fanciers call blue – is now much less common in Britain.

The British Shorthair developed from the indigenous British cats but not every shorthaired alley cat qualifies for the description. The breed that carries the name and is now accepted on the show bench has been refined by breeders to conform to very specific standards. It must be a solidly built 'cobby' (or chunky) cat with a good depth of body, level back, full broad chest, and strong short legs set on rounded paws. Its head should be round and massive with a broad skull – apple-shaped with full cheeks, a short broad nose, firm chin and small ears set well apart and rounded at the tips. Its large round eyes are orange and copper, except in white cats where they may also be blue or one blue and one orange. The coat is short and dense and the nose leather, the visible skin not covered with fur and the paw pads, as in all cat breeds, must match the coat colours: black with blue/grey coats, brick red with red, pink with cream, frosty-grey with lilac, brown with chocolate (but paw-pads may be pink), pink or matching the patching in bi-colours, and either matching the main coat colour or mingled in tortoiseshell and its variations. With colourpoints pads and nose should match the points and in

Below: Black and white Bi-colour
Left: British Silver Tipped

Below: Brown classic Tabby
Right: British Blue

tipped coats either be pink or match the tipping.

European Shorthairs are virtually identical to the British cat and judged to the same standards, although the preferences of continental judges may differ slightly.

The British Blue often has the plushest of shorthair coats and its fur and conformation most frequently approach the requirements of the British Shorthair type. At one time a dark slate colour was considered the correct colour for the fur but the present standard requires a medium to light blue, evenly shaded overall.

British breeders consider the French Chartreux breed to be identical to the British Blue. It was developed by the monks of the Abbey of Chartreuse in France, home also of the famous green liqueur. Originally it was a more massive cat than the British Blue and some American associations still make it a separate variety with a larger, less round head and larger, higher set ears. In France the eyes may be green and the fur any shade of blue.

Colours: The Exotic Shorthair is accepted in most colours and patterns – self-colours, bi-colours, tri-colours and calicos, tabbies, tipped, smoke and cameos but not in the pointed patterns. Not all American associations accept all colours. Eye colours and nose leather and paw pad colours should complement the coat as with other shorthaired cats.

Description: The Exotic Shorthair is an American breed produced by crossing American Shorthairs with Persian (Longhair) cats. From time to time the two breeds had been mated together to transfer or strengthen particular characteristics. In 1966, however, American breeders made deliberate efforts to produce a separate breed – a short-coated cat with the body type of the Persian cat. The Exotic has a cobby body with a deep chest, short, thick legs and a short tail. Its head is round, full cheeked, with a short snub nose and small ears with round tips set low on the head. The eyes are large and round.

The fur of the Exotic Shorthair is not quite so short as that of the American Shorthair but it does not tangle and is much easier to care for than the coats of the long-haired cats. It is dense, soft in texture and stands out from the body, rather than lying flat like that of the Shorthair.

EXOTIC SHORTHAIR

Below: Cream Exotic Shorthair
Left: Blue Exotic Shorthair

JAPANESE BOBTAIL

Right: Red and white Tabby

Colours: The Japanese Bobtail is recognized in most feline colours and patterns except for the agouti of the Abyssinian and Siamese points. The *mi-ke* (three-furred) white patched with black and red, is particularly popular. *Mi-ke* cats have long been considered lucky by the Japanese. The statues of the lucky *maneki-neko* (beckoning cat), famous for attracting visitors to a Tokyo shrine, depict Bobtailed cats.

Description: The Japanese Bobtail has been established in its native land for many centuries but only joined the western breeds after attracting the attention of American show judges in the 1960s. It has a short tail, only 5–13cm (2–5 in) long, which is curled back so that it looks even shorter, and with its pom-pom of fur looks rather like that of a rabbit. The genes which produce it have none of the potentially lethal effects associated with the Manx mutation – the mating of two Manx cats will result in still births.

The Japanese Bobtail is a medium-sized, well-muscled cat with longish legs and with a foreign type build. However, its medium-long head,

with high cheekbones, large, upright ears and large, oval eyes set at an angle, has a distinctive look unlike that of other foreign (or oriental) type cats. Its soft, silky fur is of medium length.

Colours: In European shows Manx and Cymric cats can be exhibited in all colours and patterns but American standards usually exclude solid-colour or patched cats with the hybrid colours chocolate and lavender (called lilac in the U.S.), and coats with Siamese-type points.

Eye colour should be appropriate to the dominant colour of the coat.

Description: Manx cats get their name from the Isle of Man in the Irish Sea but the mutation which has created this tailless cat has appeared in cats elsewhere.

The completely tailless Manx, or Rumpy, has a rump rounded like an orange, with a hollow where the tail vertebrae would normally fit in. The long rear legs carry the hindquarters high producing a characteristic rabbit-like gait. The head is like that of a British Shorthair, with a straight nose, though some American breeders prefer a definite dip in the profile. The ears are larger than in the British Shorthair and set higher on the head. The fur forms a distinctive open-textured double coat with a thick undercoat and a longer topcoat.

Cymric cats are descended from the Manx and were developed by American breeders in the 1960s. They differ from the Manx only in the length of their fur, which forms a soft, smooth coat of medium length, with tufted ears and toes and a ruff around the face.

MANX AND CYMRIC

Below: Manx Red Tabby
Left: Cymric

REX

Below: Devon Rex Tortoiseshell
Right: Blue Cream Cornish Rex

Colours: Rex cats are recognized in all the feline colours, including the Siamese pattern (often known as Si-Rex) in Britain, with chartreuse, green or yellow eyes permitted as well as colours complementary to the coat – though Si-Rex must have blue eyes. The fur is not shed much so grooming is easy. Even the whiskers of Rex are crinkled but if Devon are bred to Cornish Rex the typical Rex coat is lost.

Description: There are two types of Rex cats, Devon Rex and Cornish Rex, both developed from mutations occurring in south-west England. A mutation identical with the Cornish had previously appeared in Berlin while other forms have occurred in Ohio and Oregon. Rex cats have short, curly hair; the fur has a different balance of long, thick guard hairs, awn hairs and soft curly down hairs from that of other cats. The curly-coated Cornish has no guard hairs and in the Devon, though present, they are modified to give a short wavy coat.

Both have a foreign type build, though the Devon is full-cheeked with prominent whisker pads, large, low set, often tufted ears and a short muzzle. The Cornish has a smooth profile from ears to chin with a rather long nose, oriental eyes and a thin, whip-like tail.

Colours: Scottish Folds are recognized in America in any of the colours accepted for the American Shorthair – which excludes chocolate and lilac and their tortoiseshell variations. Any patterns combining those colours with white, and cats with a Siamese pattern coat, are also acceptable.

American Curls may also be any of the colours and patterns recognized for shorthaired cats.

Description: The Scottish Fold developed from a chance mutation in a Scottish farm cat in which the drop-down ears of the new-born kitten did not prick up as it grew. Some kittens in early litters of the breed had thickened tails and limbs which led to the Governing Council of the Cat Fancy in Britain refusing it recognition, but breeders have now been able to overcome these problems. A medium-sized cat, it has a rounded body, slender legs and tail and a rounded head with distinct whisker pads, large eyes and a short, gently curving nose. The ears should be set to give a flat, cap-like look and small, tightly folded ears are preferred.

The American Curl is a quite different and more recent mutation. It looks like the American Shorthair except for the ears which are cupped rather than upright.

SCOTTISH FOLD AND AMERICAN CURL

Below: Red Tabby American Curl
Left: Red and white Scottish Fold

SNOWSHOE

Colours: Snowshoe cats can be any of the colours recognized for other pointed cats such as the Siamese and the Birman. The Birman (page 22) has the same white gloves as the Snowshoe, but the latter has a longer head. The Snowshoe's nose leather, paw pads and skin around the eyes should complement the colour of the points. The eyes are always blue.

Description: The Snowshoe is a comparatively rare breed, created in the United States and sometimes known as Silver Laces. It combines the general sturdiness of the American Shorthair with the longer body of the oriental cats. It has oval paws and its thick tail tapers to the base. Its head is triangular in shape – but not so long as that of a Siamese – with large, oval eyes which should be a bright, sparkling blue, and large, pointed ears set fairly high on the head.

The Snowshoe has a pattern consisting of a pale coat with darker coloured face mask, lower limbs and tail, like the pointed pattern of the Siamese except that the paws themselves are white, as though the cat had walked through a dish of cream.

Colours: Although the Sphynx has no proper fur, its vestigial coat and the underlying skin carry both pigmentation and patterning. The breed is so rare that it has been recognized by only a few cat registration bodies. Hairlessness is much more important than colour, although the patterning and pigmentation of their skin perhaps appears more distinctive than when they are modified by fur.

Description: The hairless Sphynx breed is Canadian and originated in a black and white kitten born in Ontario in 1966. The lack of hair is due to a simple recessive gene which has proved difficult to breed and, since its strange appearance has not attracted a great following, it is still a rarity. Adults have a soft covering of down and some thin hairs may persist around the muzzle, on the legs and on the scrotum of toms.

Sphynx cats should have a long, hard and muscular body with a barrel-like chest, long slender neck, long tapering tail and long slim legs with neat oval paws. The head is a little longer than it is wide with a break in the smooth line of the profile above the nose and at the whisker pads. Sphynx often draw their hind legs into a 'seat' to prevent their bodies touching the ground.

BIRMAN AND RAGDOLL

Below: Birman
Right: Bi-colour Ragdoll

Colours: Birmans are recognized in Seal Point, Blue Point, Chocolate Point and Lilac Point (Lavender in the U.S.A.) by most associations; some also allow Red (Flame) Point, Tortoiseshell Point and Tabby (Lynx) Point. Nose leather is as for Siamese cats. Eyes must always be blue. Birmans must also have the characteristic white 'gloves'. Ragdolls may have the first four colourpoints only, or bicolour, and be either gloved or not.

Description: The Birman, also known as the Sacred Cat of Burma, is thought to have originated in Southeast Asia. First developed in France in the 1920s, the breed almost became extinct during the Second World War. An imported pair attracted British interest in the early 1960s and British recognition was given in 1966. America followed suit in 1967. The Birman is physically unlike other longhairs. It is well built but not so cobby as the Persian and with medium long legs, has a longer body, tail and head, and larger ears – though more rounded – than in the Siamese. It has Siamese type markings but with white paws, the white extending up the back of the lower hind legs.

The Ragdoll is a similar, strong-bodied cat, originally said to hang limp (hence the name) and be insensitive to pain – neither now considered true.

Colours: No restriction is placed on the colour and pattern of the Maine Coon and a wide range has been bred. Eye colours may be green, gold, copper, blue and their intermediate tones and any combination of coat and eye colour is permissible. Most popular is probably the brown tabby whose coat, similar to the raccoon's, helped to give the breed its name.

Description: The Maine Coon, or Maine Cat, is one of the oldest American breeds, possibly the result of breeding between domestic short-haired cats and Angoras brought to the country by early seafarers. It was long established in the State of Maine as a sturdy working cat, able to stand up to the tough, east coast winters. Popular in the 19th century, it then went out of fashion until the founding of the central Maine Coon Cat Club in 1953. Recognition and an official standard came in 1967. The CFA gave acceptance in 1977.

Large and muscular and weighing up to 13.5kg (30 lbs), the Maine Coon has a long body, long legs with large round paws, a small to medium tapering head with high cheekbones, large, slightly slanted eyes and large ears set high. The heavy, shaggy coat has a frontal ruff and the ears and toes are tufted.

MAINE COON

NORWEGIAN FOREST CAT

Below: Norwegian Forest Cat
Right: Silver Tabby

Colours: All colours are permitted in the Norwegian Forest Cat and, like the Maine Coon, they may have white colour patches on other coats which are not permissible in most other breeds. However, the breed is not very prolific and the range of colours and patterns so far bred is small compared with more widely known breeds. Much more important than colour is the possession of a double coat.

Description: The Norwegian Forest Cat, or *Norsk Skaukatt*, is a breed which naturally evolved to live in sub-Arctic conditions. It is a strong and sturdy cat with a woolly undercoat which keeps the body warm in northern winters, and with a medium-length hanging topcoat which resists rain and snow. It is somewhat similar to the Maine Coon in appearance with a longish body set on sturdy legs and a head of medium width and length with high cheekbones and large eyes set well apart. The coat is furnished with a bushy tail, full face ruff, tufted paws and feathered ears.

The breed was initially developed in the 1930s but interrupted by the Second World War. Interest revived in the 1970s and full recognition was given in 1977 by the main international organization, the *Fédération Internationale Féline*.

Colours: The Peke-faced Persian is recognized in only one colour – red; but with both red self and red tabby varieties acceptable. The eyes should be copper or orange, the nose leather and paw pads pink. This breed is not recognized in Britain.

Description: Peke-faced Persians are an extreme development of the Persian cat. They have the same cobby body, short, thick legs, shortish tail and long, luxuriant and silky fur. The head is rounded like that of the other Persians, with small wide-set ears, but the face is even more flattened with a very short nose and an indentation between the eyes. The face should resemble, to quote the CFA standard, 'as much as possible that of the Pekingese dog from which it gets its name'. The muzzle must be decidedly wrinkled and the eyes large, round and wide apart. As with Pekingese and Pug dogs, an exaggeratedly pushed-in face can cause breathing difficulties and lead to blockage or distortion of the tear ducts which breeders must take care to avoid. These risks have prevented the Peke-faced being accepted in Britain.

PEKE-FACED PERSIAN

PERSIAN (LONGHAIRED)

Below: Persian Chinchilla
Right: Golden Persian

Colours: Persian (Longhair) cats are recognized in the full range of self, tabby, bicolour, tricolour, tabby-tortoiseshell and tipped colours, and in pointed patterns too (see Himalayan). In longhair cats tabby and tortie patterns are less distinct than they appear on shorter fur. Most have orange eyes, but eyes can also be blue with white coats and emerald or aquamarine with silver and gold coats.

Himalayan is the name given to Persian cats with pale coats marked with a coloured mask and points – patterned like the Siamese – which were separated into a distinct breed by some American cat associations, although the Cat Fanciers Association now allows them to be exhibited as Persians. In Britain these are known as Colourpoint Longhairs. They include both solid, tortoiseshell and tabby (or lynx) markings.

Description: Most of today's longhaired pedigree cats are descended from cats imported to Britain from Turkey and Persia in the late 19th century. Most of these longhaired cats are of the type known popularly as Persian, although only in the United States is that name official and the various colours listed as varieties. Many years ago the British Governing Council of the Cat Fancy decided that the official name for these cats was simply Longhair and each colour was

26

classified as a separate breed.

When cat breeding and cat shows first became popular, this was the cat that attracted most enthusiasts. In a book published in 1868 Charles Ross described the Persian cat's fur as 'uniform grey on the upper part with the texture . . . as soft as silk and the lustre glossy'. When Harrison Weir began to establish standards at the end of the century, however, his standards included white, black, grey, red and 'any other' self colour cats as well as brown, blue, silver and light grey and white tabbies (perhaps what are called blue-silver today). Since then the whole range of feline colours and patterns has been introduced and a cat of very distinctive type produced.

The modern Persian, or Longhair, has a cobby, massive body, set on short, thick legs with large, round paws, a short tail carried low and a massive round head on a short, thick neck. The skull is broad with wide-set, small, round-tipped ears and a short snub nose. The fur is long and flowing over a thick undercoat with a full ruff around the face and between the forelegs. There are tufts of hair on the

Below: Black Smoke
Left: Shaded Cameo

Below: Seal Himalayan
Right: Shaded Silver

ears and between the toes and a full brush tail. A Persian cat needs help in keeping its luxuriant coat in good condition and it must be combed and groomed daily to keep it clean and tangle free.

Tipping of the long fur produces one of the most attractive coats. In the Chinchilla, for instance, each white hair in the topcoat on the head, sides and tail has a black extremity and this gives a sparkling silvery appearance to the fur. The nose is brick red but the paw pads and the visible skin of the eyelids are black, dramatically outlining the emerald or aquamarine eyes. When the black tipping extends further down each hair, so that the cat appears to wear a mantle of silver, this becomes the Shaded Silver – or in Britain, with orange instead of emerald eyes, it becomes a Pewter Longhair. If the black colour extends well down each hair with only the undercoat, near roots and a few points on the frill, flanks and eartufts left white, the cat becomes a Smoke – a coat that looks black in repose but sparkles as the cat moves and reveals the white beneath. Red tipping produces the Cameo, Shell Cameo and Cameo Red (or Red Smoke), while seal tipping produces the Shaded Golden. Chocolate, Lilac, Cream, Tortoiseshell and Blue Cream Cameos have also been created.

Colours: All the Angora cats imported into the United States from Turkey in the early 1960s were white, some with amber eyes and some with amber and blue eyes; some fanciers claim that only these are authentic Angoras, but since it has been formally adopted as a breed in America it has been accepted in most of the colours and patterns. In Britain, white, black, blue, chocolate, lilac, red, cream, tortoiseshell, blue-, chocolate- and lilac-tortie, and tabby in all colours are acceptable.

Description: Angora cats, or Turkish Angora as the American version of the breed is known, are cats with long fur, indigenous to Turkey. First taken to Western Europe in the 16th century, they were well known to 19th century fanciers, but no very clear distinction was made between them and Persians. By the 20th century they were scarcely seen outside Turkey. In 1962 a pair from Ankara Zoo was taken to the United States and Turkish Angoras were formally established there by 1970. In Britain the Angora was created from native cats.

The British Angora has a long, sinuous body with pointed head and large ears; the American is less foreign in type. The silky fur lacks the woolly undercoat of the Persian cat, making it easier to groom and keep free from tangles.

TURKISH ANGORA (ANGORA)

TURKISH VAN

Colours: The Turkish Van has a chalk white coat with auburn markings on the face and a white blaze. The ears should be white. The tail has faint auburn rings, more distinct in kittens. Some small, irregularly placed, auburn markings may occur but are not ideal. Nose leather, paw pads, eye rims and the inside of the ears should be a delicate pink. Eyes are light amber. The coat pattern has been developed in other breeds in other colours.

Description: The Turkish Van cat is an indigenous Turkish breed found in the area around Lake Van. Very similar to the Angora in its conformation, it has a long muscular body, long legs with round feet, a medium-length tail and a strong head of medium width and length which forms a wedge. The large upright ears are set fairly close together and the fur is soft and silky to the roots with no woolly undercoat. The tail is full, ears are well feathered with tufts of hair and the toes are well tufted too.

Turkish Van are active and hardy and have an affinity for water unusual in cats. Most cats instinctively swim if they have to but do not like getting wet. This breed likes to play in pools and even to swim in the sometimes ice-cold waters of its native territory.

Colours: The Abyssinian may be Usual, Sorrel (red ticked chocolate brown), blue, chocolate, lilac, fawn, red or cream (each ticked with darker colour). Tortie, silver and tortie/silver versions of these are also recognized but there are no tabby marked varieties. The Somali has not yet been accepted in so many colours and only the Usual and Sorrel are widely recognized.

Description: The Abyssinian has agouti fur, the ticked coat familiar in all tabby cats, each hair marked with two or three bands of darker colour. In the Abyssinian, however, the darker tabby pattern has largely been lost. Early examples of the breed had barring on cheeks, neck, legs, tail and underbody but a show cat today must have no trace of them.

The coat colour should shade smoothly from the belly and inside of the legs, which match the base hair

ABYSSINIAN AND SOMALI

Below: Silver Sorrel Abyssinian
Left: Abyssinian kittens

Below: Sorrel Abyssinian
Right: Blue Somali

colour (ruddy-orange or rich apricot in the original Usual or Ruddy Abyssinian), to rich golden-brown ticked black, darkest in any spinal shading. The tail tip and back of the hind legs are solid colour (black in the Usual) and there is a dark line around the eyes which have an oriental set and may be amber, hazel or green, light colour being preferred in Britain, dark in America.

A dark line extends up from the inner corner of each eye, set off by lighter fur on either side – though this is not included in the British standard. Light areas around the lips and lower jaw occur but are not desirable and must not extend onto the neck.

The origins of the Abyssinian breed are uncertain. A cat called Zulu, taken to Britain from Ethiopia in 1868, has been suggested as the ancestor of the breed even though it bears little resemblance to today's cat. Photographs taken in 1903 of Abyssinians show the modern cat. There are claims that the breed was created by British breeders from ordinary tabbies. A cat taken to Massachusetts direct from Addis Ababa in 1957, however, is said

to have looked like a true Abyssinian.

The breed is not as svelte as the Siamese. It is a medium-sized cat with slim legs on small oval feet and with a long, tapering tail. Head requirements vary in different countries but the face is rather heart shaped with large eyes and large, wide-set ears, often tufted.

The Somali is a long-haired version of the Abyssinian. It has a rather shaggy look with fur of medium length and a full tail brush. Its full ticking takes a long time to develop but there may be up to 12 bands.

Colours: In America only sable brown cats are recognized by the Cat Fanciers Association as Burmese and some other registration bodies limit recognition to brown (sable), blue, chocolate (champagne) and lilac (platinum). In Britain and countries following the British standard, red and cream solid colours and tortoiseshell coats are also accepted as Burmese.

The Malayan cat is identical in all respects except colour to the Burmese cat of American type. Some registration bodies apply the name to the red, cream and tortoiseshell variations of coat colour, and the Cat Fanciers Association uses it for all colours except the original sable Burmese. The breed does not exist in Britain, where all the colours qualify for recognition as Burmese.

Description: The Burmese breed has its origin in a cat taken to the United States from Rangoon in 1930, now known to have been a hybrid Siamese. Mated to Siamese, it produced some normal Siamese, some with less distinct points (Tonkinese) and others more evenly dark – the first Burmese,

BURMESE AND MALAYAN

Left: Platinum Burmese

Below: Malayan
Right: Lilac Burmese

recognized as a breed in 1936. Frequent breeding to Siamese emphasized the Siamese look and for a time registration was suspended, but by 1953 they had returned to type. This is now established in America as a substantial cat with a round head, full face, yellow-to-gold round eyes and round paws.

In Britain the breed was developed from cats imported from America which were very much of the Siamese type. It was this which became the standard when the brown Burmese was recognized by the GCCF in 1952. The British form of the Burmese therefore must be more oriental in conformation than would be acceptable in the United States. Its eyes, which may range from chartreuse to amber, are rounded below but slanting above.

All Burmese have a short, dense coat of fine, glossy fur which shades to a slightly paler colour on the belly. From the original brown-coated cat a number of other colours have been developed. Blue first appeared in Britain, where it was recognized in 1960. Only some colours are recognized as

Burmese by the American registration bodies; the others are given the name Malayan. Kittens are usually born with much paler fur and it may not be easy to determine their precise colour until they are a few weeks old.

There is a long-haired version of the Burmese known as the Tiffany (see title page).

Colours: The Mau is recognized in silver (charcoal markings on pale silver), bronze (dark chocolate on light bronze), smoke (jet black on charcoal grey with silver undercoat), and pewter (charcoal to dark brown on fawn banded with silver and beige and tipped black). The eyes are a pale gooseberry green with all coat colours.

Description: Mau is the ancient Egyptian word for the domesticated cat. The Egyptian Mau is believed to be a natural breed which first appeared in Europe in the early 1950s and was then exported to the U.S.A. Recognition of the breed in that country came in 1968.

It has an oriental build combined with a rather cobby body. The head is a slightly rounded wedge, ears are medium to large, eyes large and almond shaped and midway between round and oriental. The spotted coat is silky and long enough to carry two or more bands of ticking. The cheeks are barred and the forehead marked with an M, with lines traversing the head to break into spots on the spine before becoming a dorsal stripe. The chest has broken 'necklaces', the legs are barred, the tail ringed and the haunches and shoulders have bars breaking into spots.

EGYPTIAN MAU

Left: Silver-spotted Mau

HAVANA BROWN (HAVANA)

Below: Havana Brown
Right: Foreign Black

Colours: The Havana Brown has a smooth coat of medium length which must be a rich warm mahogany brown in colour, with the entire coat the same shade right down to the skin. Even the whiskers should be brown. The nose leather should be rose and the oval eyes chartreuse.

This is a one-colour breed and there are no other colour varieties.

Description: The Havana was first bred in Britain in the early 1950s and was the result of a Seal Point Siamese crossed to a black shorthaired cat of Siamese lineage. The name 'Havana' is derived from a breed of rabbit with similar fur, although it was originally called a Chestnut Foreign Shorthair by the GCCF on its recognition of the breed in 1958.

The Havana has a long, wedge-shaped head, large, slightly pointed ears and a firm chin; its body is long and muscular.

Early examples of the breed with less Siamese characteristics were exported to the U.S.A. from which a quite separate breed, the Havana Brown, was developed and rapidly accepted. It was recognized in 1959.

The Havana Brown differs from the British Havana by having a rounder muzzle, a stop at the eyes, a slight break behind the whiskers and large, round-tipped ears.

Colours: The short, single-layered coat of the Korat may be any shade of blue. It is even and without ghost markings, and with a silver tipping which develops through kittenhood to full intensity at about two years old. Nose leather and paw pads should be blue, the eyes a brilliant green, although an amber cast is acceptable, and kittens and adolescents have yellow or amber to amber-green eyes.

Description: The Korat, or 'Si-Sawat' as it is known in its native Thailand, is one of the oldest natural breeds. It is believed to have been named after the Thai province where it originated. The breed did not take its place in the West until a pair of them was imported into the United States in 1959. Recognition in that country was given in 1966 but not until 1975 was it granted in Britain.

The Korat is medium-sized, neither as svelte as the Siamese or as cobby as the Shorthairs, with slender legs and a tapering tail. Its head is heart-shaped with large, high-set, round-tipped ears, a slight break between nose and forehead and the sides curving gently down to the chin. The eyes are large – oversized for the face – full round when open, with an oriental slant when partly closed.

OCICAT AND BENGALI

Below: Ocicat
Right: Silver Ocicat

Colours: The Ocicat can be dark chestnut (dark markings on creamy beige), light chestnut (milk chocolate on creamy beige), silver (charcoal on pale silver) or bronze (dark brown on light bronze). The Bengali has an attractive light bronze coat with dark brown markings. As with all relatively new breeds it is possible to develop a variety of new colours.

Description: The Ocicat is a recent American breed, so named because its appearance reminded breeders of a young ocelot. Abyssinian, Siamese and American Shorthair blood are all present in its makeup, producing a large and muscular cat. Its short, silky coat has a pattern similar to that of the Egyptian Mau.

The Bengali is another American-bred spotted cat with face and body markings like those of the Asian Leopard Cat from which it was developed. Male hybrids from crosses between domestic cats and the wild species proved sterile but the females were mated first to a feral cat found in the rhino compound at Delhi Zoo which was red with brown rosettes, then to a brown spotted tabby from Los Angeles to produce an attractive animal with horizontal lines of spots.

Colours: As well as the colours common to the Shorthair and Persian cats, a whole range of other self colours have been developed in the Oriental Shorthair, including cinnamon, fawn, beige, apricot, caramel and indigo. These may also be applied to tipped, tabby, bi-colour and tri-colour patterns, with silver and golden shading. Spotted patterns have proved particularly popular with breeders.

Description: Oriental Shorthairs, or Foreign Shorthairs as they are also known, are basically Siamese cats which have an all-over coat instead of carrying the dark Siamese points. They also have the same lively but demanding character.

Among the first to be recognized were the Foreign White (White Oriental Shorthair), which retains the blue eyes of the Siamese (although in America it may also have green eyes), the Foreign Lilac (Lavender Oriental), which has green eyes, and the Foreign Black (Ebony Oriental) also with green eyes, with amber also allowed in America. These, together with the Blue (green eyes), Red (copper to green), Cream (copper to cream), and other self colours (all green-eyed) are classed as Foreign Shorthairs in Britain, only the patterned and tipped cats being called Oriental – as they are all known in America.

ORIENTAL (FOREIGN) SHORTHAIR

Below: Oriental Shorthair
Left: Oriental Spotted Tabby

RUSSIAN BLUE

Below: Russian White
Right: Russian Blue

Colours: The Russian Blue has a short thick double coat which stands away from the body. It should be a clear, even blue throughout and free from shading or tabby markings. The guard hairs are silver tipped. Lighter shades are preferred in America, and with slate grey nose leather and lavender, pink or mauve paw pads. A medium blue is accepted in Britain with blue nose and paw pads. A Russian White and a Russian Black have also been bred.

Description: The origin of the Russian Blue is uncertain, although there is good evidence that it is a natural Russian breed. Examples were said to have been brought to Britain from the Russian port of Archangelsk by Elizabethan sailors and it was known at first as the Archangel cat. Later it was known as the Maltese cat, particularly in the U.S.A. in the early 1900s.

In Britain it shared a class with the British Blue until 1912, then becoming a breed in its own right. It declined during the Second World War and attempts to revive it by introducing Siamese blood led to the virtual disappearance of the original type of breed.

Efforts by breeders on both sides of the Atlantic in the 1960s led to its return.

Today's Russian Blue is long and graceful with a short, wedge-shaped head. The British type has oval feet, large, high-set ears and vivid green, almond eyes; the American type has round feet and eyes and less oriental ears.

Colours: Siamese points may be seal, blue, chocolate, lilac (lavender), red or cream. The cat also appears in tabby (lynx) and tortoiseshell versions of these colours. Body colours should be, respectively, cream shading to pale fawn on the back, glacial white, ivory, off white (magnolia), white shading to apricot on the back and white shading to pale cream. All Siamese cats should have intense blue eyes.

Description: The origins of the Siamese cat are uncertain. Evidence that it may have originated in Thailand comes partly in the form of an early (pre-1676) manuscript held in the National Library, Bangkok, called *Cat Book Poems*, which depicts Siamese-type pointed cats with pale coats marked with dark lower limbs, tail, ears and a face mask. The German naturalist Simon Pallas reported seeing a darker type of pointed cat east of the Caspian Sea in 1793 (temperature affects the depth of Siamese colour and this may have been a variant due to the cooler climate).

Siamese cats had been taken to Britain by 1871 and to the United States by 1890. They had become a popular breed by the end of the century, although these cats were much rounder than today's.

The modern Siamese is a slim, elegant cat with a long body set on fine limbs and with oval paws and a long and tapering tail. It has a long, wedge-shaped head with large pointed ears, wide at the base, and slightly sloping almond-shaped eyes of brilliant blue. The coloured points develop in the first months of a

SIAMESE

Below: Siamese Seal Point
Left: Siamese Blue Point

Below: Siamese Lilac Tabby
Right: Siamese Tortie Point

kitten's life and in a mature cat should be clearly defined, with the face mask spreading out from the nose and connected by tracings with the ears. The fur is short and fine, glossy and close lying and easy to groom. Siamese are lively and intelligent cats, often talkative with humans – though some people find their voices harsh (especially the female when in oestrus) – and they can be very demanding companions.

At first only Seal was accepted – dark brown points – but a wide range of colours is now bred. However, some American associations accept only Seal, Blue, Chocolate and Lilac (Lavender) points as Siamese. These associations place cats of a Siamese type and pattern in other colours or with tabby and tortoiseshell points in a separate breed called Colorpoint Shorthairs.

Colours: The Balinese may be any of the colours recognized for Siamese cats but American associations recognize only the four basic Siamese colours. Other colours and tabby and tortoiseshell points are known as Javanese. In New Zealand and some other places Javanese applies to similar but unpointed cats. All have blue eyes.

Description: Balinese cats were developed from the occasional long-haired kittens that appear in Siamese litters and which had previously been rejected by breeders. The name of the breed was chosen because the cat's grace and beauty were said to be reminiscent of Balinese dancers.

The Balinese is in all respects like a Siamese cat except for the length of its fur, which is long and silky, though lying close to the body, and without a woolly undercoat. The tail should form a plume and the ears should be tufted.

BALINESE AND JAVANESE

Below: Javanese
Left: Balinese kitten

SINGAPURA AND BOMBAY

Below and right: Singapura

Colours: The Singapura is sepia agouti (dark brown ticking on warm ivory) with muzzle, chin, chest and underparts ecru, ears and bridge of nose salmon-toned. Nose leather is salmon-outlined dark brown. Eye rims are dark brown and paw pads rosy brown. The eyes are hazel-green or yellow.

The Bombay is jet black and its large, round eyes are gold. There are no other colour forms.

Description: The Singapura, recently developed in America from cats discovered in Singapore, is small to medium sized, its stocky body set on fairly heavy legs that taper to oval paws and with a medium-length, blunt-tipped tail. The rather rounded head has large, slightly pointed ears, large, almond-shaped eyes, a blunt nose, a definite whisker break and a well formed chin. The fur is short and dark at the tip with at least two bands of dark ticking. The tip of the tail is dark with the shading continuing along the top of the tail.

The Bombay, another American breed, resulting from crossing Burmese with black American Shorthairs, was recognized in 1976. It has the physique of the American Shorthair, but a Burmese head and the sleek Burmese coat.

TONKINESE

Colours: The Tonkinese is bred in Natural Mink (Seal), Blue Mink, Honey Mink (Chocolate), Champagne (Lilac), Platinum, colours of tortoiseshell, tabby and torbie. Not all are recognized by all registration bodies, however, and some associations recognize only the first five colours. The eyes are a rich blue-green colour.

Description: When the Rangoon cat Wong Mau was mated with Siamese to produce the Burmese breed, some offspring appeared with points, though less distinctly marked than the Siamese. These were intermediate between Siamese and Burmese and the type was known as Tonkinese. Mating Siamese and Burmese produces the same type, but the American Burmese must be used, as the British is too Siamese looking to produce the correct result. Mating two Tonkinese may produce all three types in the litter.

The Tonkinese is a slim cat of medium size with slim legs and oval paws. The head is a modified wedge with almond-shaped eyes, more open than in the modern Siamese. The rich, even colour of the fur, darker at the points, may take a year and a half to develop from a kitten's paler coat.

45

THE NEW BREEDS

Below: Black-tipped Burmilla
Right: Burmilla

Colours: The ground colour of the Burmilla may be silver or golden with tipping in Black (Sepia), Blue, Chocolate (Mocha), Lilac (Dove), Caramel (Taupe), Beige (Flax), Red (Magenta), Cream (Parchment), and Apricot (Ivory). The eyes may be any shade of green.

Spotted Mists may be spotted Brown, Blue, Chocolate, Lilac and Gold (Caramel), always on a creamish mushroom background.

Description: The Burmilla, a British breed which originated in a chance mating between a Chinchilla and a lilac Burmese, has a rounded head with Burmese eyes, slim legs with oval paws and a medium tail with rounded tip.

The Spotted Mist, an Australian breed, was developed from domestic, Abyssinian and Burmese cats. It is like a British shorthair but with a soft, dense, Burmese coat in a misty, ticked ground colour patterned with subtle spots.

Newer breeds include: British Burmoire, developed from Burmilla and Burmese, of Burmese type but with a coat like Oriental smokes; Asian tabby, similar with an Oriental ticked tabby coat; Seychellois, a white-coated Oriental splashed with colour – in long- and short-haired forms; and the Californian Spangled, a spotted cat developed in America.